LET'S GET A PET!

MY FIRST HAMSTER

By Joan Stoltman

 Gareth Stevens
PUBLISHING

Please visit our website, www.garethstevens.com. For a free color catalog of all our high-quality books, call toll free 1-800-542-2595 or fax 1-877-542-2596.

Library of Congress Cataloging-in-Publication Data

Names: Stoltman, Joan.
Title: My first hamster / Joan Stoltman.
Description: New York : Gareth Stevens Publishing, 2018. | Series: Let's get a pet! | Includes index.
Identifiers: ISBN 9781482464573 (pbk.) | ISBN 9781482464597 (library bound) | ISBN 9781482464580 (6 pack)
Subjects: LCSH: Hamsters as pets–Juvenile literature.
Classification: LCC SF459.H3 S76 2017 | DDC 636.935–dc23

Published in 2018 by
Gareth Stevens Publishing
111 East 14th Street, Suite 349
New York, NY 10003

Copyright © 2018 Gareth Stevens Publishing

Designer: Bethany Perl
Editor: Joan Stoltman

Photo credits: Cover, p. 1 CRISTINA TIUREAN/Shutterstock.com; pp. 2-24 (background texture) Liliya Mulyukova/Shutterstock.com; p. 5 (main image) Monkey Business Images/Shutterstock.com; p. 5 (hamster) Elya Vatel/Shutterstock.com; p. 7 Vyaseleva Elena/Shutterstock.com; p. 9 Domnich Vladislav/Shutterstock.com; p. 11, 19 fantom_rd/Shutterstock.com; p. 13 Dorling Kindersley/Getty Images; p. 15 (hamster wheel, wooden house) Andy Lidstone/Shutterstock.com; p. 15 (hamster ball) Africa Studio/Shutterstock.com; p. 15 (hamster house) gulserinak1955/Shutterstock.com; p. 17 Jerome Wexler/Science Source/Getty Images; p. 21 Natalia7/Shutterstock.com.

Printed in China

CPSIA compliance information: Batch #CS17GS: For further information contact Gareth Stevens, New York, New York at 1-800-542-2595.

CONTENTS

Boldface words appear in the glossary.

Hamsters Are Great!

Hamsters make great pets! They clean themselves. They're easy to train with food. They're commonly friendly and like people. However, it may take a few weeks or months for your hamster to feel safe in its new home.

Getting to Know You

Hamsters will bite when scared. Give your new pet time to get used to you. After a few days of just talking to it, let your hamster smell your hand. Then, put a treat in your hand, and let your hamster come over.

After a few days of treats, try to pick up your hamster. Make a hand cave, letting it stick its head out. It might pee on you if it's nervous. Put it back in its cage, and be **patient**. You'll be friends soon enough!

An Interesting Body!

Hamsters can hardly see at all! But they make up for that with amazing senses of hearing and smell. They also have big cheek pouches. They store food inside their cheek pouches so they can move it to a safe place to eat. How cool!

CHEEK
POUCH

11

Asleep

Hamsters mostly sleep all day, but will wake up a few times to eat and drink. They make their own beds! They'll gather **material** from their cage, just like a bird finding sticks and grasses for a nest.

13

Awake

Hamsters get very busy at **twilight**. They'll want to climb, run, eat, **burrow**, and tunnel! They'll also want to chew. Their four front teeth are always growing, just like our fingernails! They need safe chew toys to keep those teeth from getting too long.

KEEPING BUSY

HAMSTER BALL

WOODEN TOY

HAMSTER HOUSE

HAMSTER WHEEL

Cage Setup

Hamsters need a quiet room with little light. They're good at climbing up, but not down. When setting up their cage, make sure they can't fall off anything too high! Attach a water bottle to the cage so they always have something to drink.

Chow Time!

Hamsters like to eat a little throughout the day and night. They need fresh food each time they eat. They'll also put food in their cheek pouches and hide it for later. This food can rot, so clean their cage weekly.

Hamsters can eat seeds, grasses, fruits, vegetables, and even cooked eggs! Ask an adult before giving your hamster new food. In nature, they eat bugs. You can buy live mealworms and crickets at the pet store as a special treat!

GLOSSARY

burrow: a hole made by an animal in which it lives or hides

material: something used to make something, such as a fabric

patient: able to wait a long time

twilight: the time of the day just after the sun sets and just before the sun rises

READ MORE INFORMATION

BOOKS

Ganeri, Anita. *Nibble's Guide to Caring for Your Hamster.* Chicago, IL: Capstone Heinemann Library, 2013.

Gardeski, Christina Mia. *Hamsters: Questions and Answers.* North Mankato, MN: Capstone Press, 2017.

Thomas, Isabel. *Hip Hamster Projects.* Chicago, IL: Heinemann Raintree, 2016.

WEBSITES

Harry the Hamster Game
petgames.my-pet-care.com/hamster-games/harry-the-hamster.html
Play this fun online hamster game!

How to Be a Good Hamster Owner
www.wikihow.com/Be-a-Good-Hamster-Owner-(for-Kids)
Read these 10 steps to improve your hamster-owning skills!

The Hamster House
thehamsterhouse.com
Read all sorts of articles about hamsters!

INDEX